The Anti Racist Teacher
Reading Instruction Workbook

By Lorena Germán

United States
2020

Author: Lorena Germán

Printed in the United States of North America

ISBN: 9781677474226

Book design: Wanda Estévez

Cover design: Wanda Estévez

Welcome!

Thank you for taking a step in this journey. Whether you've been digging in this work before, or this is your first step, welcome. Angela Davis tells us that, "In a racist society, it's not enough to be non-racist, we must be anti racist." We should all be engaged in this process of becoming anti-racist. For some of us it means probing deep within ourselves to find the ways that we've internalized the racism cloaked over us and used to oppress us. For some of you, it means analyzing how your behavior is steeped in White supremacy and upholding the systems your ancestors designed. Regardless of how you walk into the work, we know there is work to do.

Recently, Teaching Tolerance (a project of the Southern Poverty Law Center) published the "Hate at School Report." The findings of the report are astounding and painful to read. The results are part of the impetus for this workbook and the work we should be committed to. Did you know that in 2017 about 35% of students reported being worried and anxious about hate and bias at school? Did you know that when teachers discriminate against students those students question their academic abilities and belonging at school? Did you know that racial and ethnic hate and bias are often experienced in the form of "slurs and racist iconography"? Did you know that over 60% of hate and bias incidents happen at the middle and high school level and that over 30% of those incidents occur in the classroom? I didn't.

Determining that you are anti racist is crucial. The step after determining that, is determining what you do stand for. If you're against racism, then what are you for? I find that when we talk about anti-racism, we are rarely including colonialism as part of the root of the problem. Racism began when Europeans had the idea that they could travel to another land, take it, and dispossess (then murder) the people of that land. Therefore, anti-Indigenous colonialism must be a central part of the conversation and effort of anti-racism. In my growth, I've learned that when I talk about anti racism I mean: racial equity, racial justice, redistribution of power, reparations, and rebuilding. All of the institutions and systems in this country need to be rebuilt. Until then, we inspect and correct.

I hope that as educators we believe in the potential and power of the young people sitting in front of us. That's how we ended up in this work, right? We believe that they really are the ones that will either change this country or maintain the current racist status quo we're living in. There are many factors playing a role in what they'll become, and educators are one of them. We are one of those factors that has the power to inspire them to see differently and act boldly. We cannot underestimate our impact as teachers.

There are so many aspects to being a reading instructor. So much of what we do comes from a pre-existing structure and system that we were educated in. There are actions we take and beliefs we hold as reading instructors that we didn't necessarily choose for ourselves. There were, and continue to be, so many practices I'm revisiting and undoing myself. I'm not above this work. My sleeves are up and I'm digging in, too.

And so, **The Anti Racist Teacher:** Reading Instruction Workbook is for everybody. We all have to do this work. I want Latinxs, African Americans, Black Americans, Asians, Asian Americans, and Indigenous people of this land to reconsider and evaluate themselves using this workbook. Whose values are we holding onto tightly and how are those values impacting young people? I was thinking of you as I worked on this. I did this because I love you; because I love us. White folks, we need you, too. As descendants of colonizers, you have so much undoing to take on. The work before you is critical and essential. This is not about shame. Take that pain and turn it into a fierce love for justice and righteousness.

Table of contents

The purpose of The Anti Racist Teacher:
Reading Instruction Workbook is for reading teachers
to have a resource we can turn to in order to do necessary
introspective anti racist work. Second, it's purpose is to
create a community for us.
Progress and liberation won't happen in isolation.
The movement toward racial justice and equity will only
happen in community.
Thank you for joining this community. Thank you
for considering this workbook in your journey. Let's dig in.
There's so much work to do.

Before we begin…

I'm going to be using terms throughout this workbook that may be new to you. I want to take the time to define those here, so we're on the same page.

White gaze

This phrase refers to the White-centered/Eurocentric vision that dominates White American society. In the case of this workbook, I am talking about the presence of White-centered literature and texts. It is a world-view where the audience is assumed to be White, where plots and lives are for White people to understand and consume.

People of the Global Majority/People of Color (PoGM/PoC)

This is a term I use to refer to who we all call People of Color. I use that term so that we can keep in mind the truth that we are a global majority. It also shifts the dynamic of thinking that we are 'minorities' or that we are less than.

White Supremacy

This is the belief at the root of our system that holds that Whiteness/White race as superior to other ways of being and existing. It is at the foundation of all institutions in this country.

Pedagogy(ies)

Pedagogy, by definition, is the craft of teaching. Scholars often use this term to encompass praxis, or practice of teaching. This is why we can use it in the plural, because it's really a set of crafts and practices.

Traits of White Supremacy Culture
IN READING INSTRUCTION
Adapted from Tema Okun

Tema Okun, a White woman, developed a list of traits that define White Supremacy culture. It's interesting to read them because as an insider to White culture, she has extensive knowledge. She describes how these traits show up in organizations. I want to invite us to think about how they're present in our ELA classrooms. Culture is powerful because it shapes our entire life. Yet, it's difficult to pin down. Below is a list of the traits Tema Okun identified:

- Perfectionism
- Sense of urgency
- Defensiveness
- Quantity over quality
- Worship of the written word
- Paternalism
- Either/or thinking
- Power hoarding
- Fear of open conflict
- Individualism
- Progress is bigger, more
- Objectivity
- Right to comfort

What I appreciate about her work is that she focuses on how all of this builds a culture. It's not about an individual, but a collective. While all of these could be expanded upon to analyze reading instruction, I have selected seven I wanted us to focus on. I have adapted their definitions and explanations in order to think about them through the lens of reading instruction.

One of the biggest challenges of accepting the truth of these traits is how we might see them as social norms because 'this is how it's always been.' We might even want to reject them as racialized, because they seem so 'universal'. But we must be self-critical and openly evaluate these ideas because they promote White Supremacy thinking; they promote the violent harm that is at the foundation of our country. We agree that all early colonizers were racists, and we must therefore agree that their shared values and beliefs were also racist. Their behaviors can be attributed to their values, and those values are directly connected to the traits listed above. In the graphic below I analyze an early colonizer by making direct connections between these traits and his behaviors.

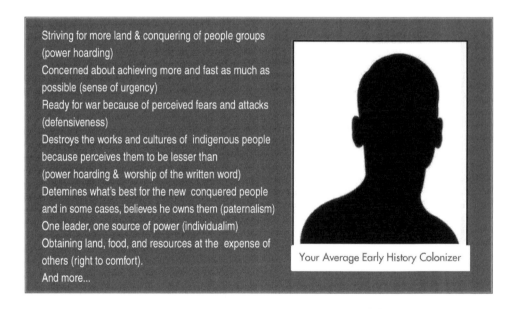

Striving for more land & conquering of people groups (power hoarding)
Concerned about achieving more and fast as much as possible (sense of urgency)
Ready for war because of perceived fears and attacks (defensiveness)
Destroys the works and cultures of indigenous people because perceives them to be lesser than (power hoarding & worship of the written word)
Detemines what's best for the new conquered people and in some cases, believes he owns them (paternalism)
One leader, one source of power (individualim)
Obtaining land, food, and resources at the expense of others (right to comfort).
And more...

Your Average Early History Colonizer

My point is that the aspects of our culture that we think are common sense and good practice, are purely subjective and based on our context. Okun explains that, "Because we all live in a White Supremacy culture, these characteristics show up in the attitudes and behaviors of all of us – People of Color and White people.

Therefore, these attitudes and behaviors can show up in any group or organization, whether it is White-led, or predominantly White, or People of Color-led, or predominantly People of Color." Similarly for us, these beliefs are embedded in our educational system and pedagogical practices.

TRAIT: PERFECTIONISM

- Little appreciation or positive feedback is expressed among students for the work that others are doing.
- Appreciation that is expressed is usually directed to students already considered fast or strong readers
- It is more common to point to someone's mistakes when reading or their inadequacy as readers
- A classroom culture where students discuss others' reading skills or abilities behind their back (gossip)
- Reading mistakes are perceived as personal (they reflect badly on the person making them) as opposed to being seen for what they are: mistakes
- Reading instruction that too often tends to identify what's wrong and little ability to identify, name, and appreciate what's right

A student in this classroom receiving this type of instruction may internalize these ideas of perfectionism in terms of their reading identity.
They may exhibit the following reading attitudes:

- Self-identifying as a perfectionist as a positive trait and failing to appreciate their own reading progress
- They often point out their failures and the shortcomings of their peers
- They hyperfocus on their inadequacies about reading, completing readings, and comprehension

Ways to dismantle perfectionism in reading instruction:

- Develop a reading culture of appreciation where students' skills and abilities are celebrated
- Help students know that mistakes are expected and are opportu nities for growth
- Mistakes are seen as separate from the person not as defining traits
- Consider offering positive feedback before feedback identifying areas

of growth and truly celebrate students with substantive observations
• Openly talk about reading discomfort and demystifying fears

Below are sentence starters you can use with students to openly talk about reading discomforts & demystifying fears.

Something that makes me uncomfortable when I'm reading is...
A discomfort I have when reading aloud is...
I'm afraid to .... when reading because...
Reading causes me to feel....

TRAIT: SENSE OF URGENCY

• A continued sense of urgency that makes it difficult to take the necessary time to include others in the reading process or consider the various levels or speed of reading.
• A whole class reading experience where the reading should be fast and students are not offered to read at their own pace.
• The sense of urgency doesn't allow the teacher to engage students in discussion of nuanced, difficult topics because they must focus on "test-taking" skills, for example.
• Novels and texts are read quickly in order to get to the work that must be completed. It becomes about reading to complete vs. reading to empathize.

A student in this classroom receiving this type of instruction may internalize a sense of urgency in terms of their reading identity. They may exhibit the following reading attitudes:
• Always feel rushed to complete work because completion is more important than quality
• Pride themselves in speed when turning in work
• Feel frustrated when they don't achieve goals by a predetermined deadline and then deal with mistakes negatively (as mentioned in perfectionism)

Ways to dismantle a sense of urgency in reading instruction:

- Understand that reading, comprehension, and analysis take time and are a cyclical process, unbound by an exam
- Taking time to discuss students' reader identities and emotions related to reading
- Be clear with students about the time constraints you do have and have an open dialogue about what you will attempt to achieve

Below is an excerpt of a chart I've used before with students to help them explore their reader identities and reading-related emotions:

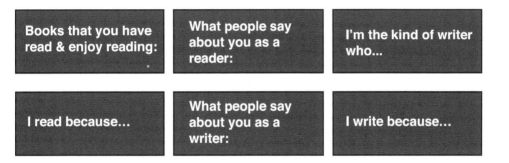

| Books that you have read & enjoy reading: | What people say about you as a reader: | I'm the kind of writer who... |
| I read because... | What people say about you as a writer: | I write because... |

TRAIT: DEFENSIVENESS

- The act of reading is highly monitored and much energy is spent trying to prevent kids from not following the reading rules rather than promoting a love of reading and student choice
- Responses to new or challenging ideas, authors, genres, and/or forms with defensiveness, making it very difficult to make suggestions that promote diversity
- Teachers spend energy defending against charges of racism instead of examining how racism is actually happening
- Teachers perceive calls for change as personal attacks

A student in this classroom receiving this type of instruction may internalize defensiveness in terms of their reading identity. They may exhibit the follo-wing reading attitudes:

- The students believe that they cannot make suggestions for new titles or share interests in voices other than the ones represented in the teachers' curriculum.

• These students may see an attack on 'classical' texts as personal attacks and negative critiques without considering value in differing points of view.

Ways to dismantle defensiveness in reading instruction:
  • Understanding that defensiveness is connected to fear of losing power, make space for yourself and for your students to consider books (and all forms of text) outside of what is considered the literary canon.
  • Name defensiveness as a problem when it is one and work on your own defensiveness.
  • Engage with students in a conversation about how defensiveness of the canon has allowed for marginalized voices to be historically ex cluded from classrooms.

Addressing defensiveness can take place in varioous ways.
I often do this through 1-1 conversations with students. I use questions such as the ones on the right.

• Are you noticing your defensiveness right now? What is making you feel this way and why do you think that is?

• Why is this bringing up discomfort for you and why is letting that go so hard?

• How can I support you to tackle the defensiveness you're feeling right now?

TRAIT: QUANTITY OVER QUALITY
  • Your reading instruction prioritizes producing measurable goals
  • Tasks that can be measured are more highly valued than tasks that cannot be measured or quantified
  • There is little to no value attached to process; if it can't be measured, it has no value
  • How many books are more important than what types of books students are reading, or how meaningful they may be

A student in this classroom receiving this type of instruction may internalize a sense of quantity over quality in terms of their reading identity.
They may exhibit the following reading attitudes:
- They prioritize the number of pages they've read over comprehension
- They prioritize the number of books they've read over comprehension
- They emphasize reading speed (also sense of urgency)

Ways to dismantle a sense of urgency in reading instruction:
- Create space for students to value process, slowing down, and meaning over number of pages or books completed
- Take breaks in the unit to respond to needs and to process reading the book(s) with students

Below are some sentence starters you can use to pause and process the reading with students:

How is the reading making you feel?
Is the text bringing up big feelings about ___? Why or why not?
How might this text be trying to dig into our lives and our past histories?
I'm feeling ___. Is anyone else having similar thoughts?

TRAIT: WORSHIP OF THE WRITTEN WORD

- If it's not a 'traditional' book in print, it doesn't count as reading
- Other forms of reading and texts are not valued or welcomed
- Teachers mainly celebrate students with abilities to read quickly and students whose preferences include the 'traditional classical' texts
- Only a certain type of language is honored or respected and is the only one allowed to exist in the classroom.
- The only books taught are the ones using Dominant American English as well as British English and any book containing any other form of English is discounted and critiqued.

A student in this classroom receiving this type of instruction may internalize a worship of the written word in terms of their reading identity. They may exhibit the following reading attitudes:

- Negative perception of books or texts that feature a variety of Englishes such as African American Vernacular English or Spanglish
- Valuing 'classical' literature as the only 'real literature'
- Closed-minded attitude toward books in verse, graphic novels, books by authors of color, etc

Ways to dismantle a worship of the written word in reading instruction:

- Incorporate texts and books that feature various types of formats and Englishes
- Consider incorporating visual texts and visual analyses

TEXT	WHAT IT CONTAINS
Citizen (Rankine 2014)	Poetry, visual media, prose
The Forgetting Tree (Paris 2017)	Essays, pictures, poems, prose, African American Vernacular English
Puerto Rico Strong (Newlevant, Rodriguez 2018)	Graphic novel prose, poems, memoir, and fiction, Spanglish

TRAIT: ONLY ONE RIGHT WAY

- The belief that there is one right way to read and consume a text and once students learn that method, they'll use it forever
- When students don't adopt or use the teacher's methods, they are perceived to be a problem
- Students are expected to process texts one way (for example: annotating, highlighting, or using post it's)
- Reading assessments don't allow for various modes of demon strating student learning

A student in this classroom receiving this type of instruction may internalize only-one-right-way thinking in terms of their reading identity. They may exhibit the following reading attitudes:

- Reading only happens in class or in designated spaces the teacher has identified
- They don't seem to be independent or choice readers, but simply comply with the teacher's reading instructions

Ways to dismantle the 'only one right way' value in reading instruction:

- Allow students freedom of choice when they read and how they process that reading
- Notice what students do when they read and consider adopting those methods or offering them to other students as options
- Keep in mind that you serve students, so learning about them and their ways is crucial to helping them develop as readers

TRAIT: INDIVIDUALISM

- The idea that readers process texts alone
- Ignoring the socio political context of the readers in the room to analyze what they're reading, what biases they hold as readers of that specific book, and the historical and political time and place of their reading it
- Celebration for individual students who complete books "on their own"
- Reading competitions are valued and celebrated rather than coopera tion and reading as a community
- 'Independent reading time' becomes a veil for students to get their work done alone at the expense of community building time or teacher-stu dent rapport-building

A student in this classroom receiving this type of instruction may internalize a value for individualism in terms of their reading identity. They may exhibit the following reading attitudes:

• Believes that reading happens alone and books are read in isolation

Ways to dismantle individualism in reading instruction:

• Include partner reading and community reading as an important value and method to reading instruction

• Help students to evaluate and analyze their reader identity and sociopolitical context, including their biases

Below is a process chart showing how you can include partner and community readings to process a text.

In partners, students read the excerpt.

With partners, trn to another partner set and discuss the reading.

Turn to the whole class and bring up points of discussion and analysis.

Okay, now breathe.

One of the benefits of analyzing the traits of White Supremacy culture is to be able to tackle the ways our practices are unconsciously making it impossible for our students to work toward liberation. When we don't do this work, our push for equity or our desires to be anti-racist are just that: pushes and desires. They're not actionable. Being able to name the practices, the details, the "little things" that make the big thing operate is one way to deconstruct it all and dismantle the monster that is racism. We have to start with ourselves.

Culturally Sustaining Pedagogies
REFLECTION EXERCISE

Below are quotes from Dr. Django Paris and Dr. Samy Alim's book Culturally Sustaining Pedagogies (2018 Teachers College Press). After the quotes, are reflection questions to help us think about application.

Note to reader: If you're not reading this book, then please know that Dr. Gloria Ladson-Billings is a supporter of CSP, her work is foundational to their work, she's shown deep respect in this chapter, and she authors a chapter later in the textbook, which is unequivocal fire.

"The purpose of "state-sanctioned" education has been to assimilate students and enact a violent, White-centered ideology." [1]

"CSP seeks to perpetuate and foster- to sustain- linguistic, literate, and cultural pluralism as part of the schooling for positive social transformation." [1]

"CSP exists when educators are intentionally sustaining the lifeways of communities who have been historically (and continue to be) oppressed through schooling." [1]

"There is a fallacy to measuring ourselves/students of color against White middle class norms that dictate success and normalcy."

"The term relevant (from culturally relevant teaching) does not do enough to explicitly support the goals of maintenance and social critique. It is quite possible to be relevant to something without ensuring its continuing and critical presence in students' repertoire of practice and its presence in our classrooms and communities." [5]

"For too long we have taught our youth (and our teachers) that Dominant American English (DAE) and other White middle-class normed practices and ways of being are the key to power, while denying the languages and other cultural practices that students of color bring to the classroom. Ironically, this outdated philosophy will not grant our young people access to power; rather, it may increasingly deny them that access." [6]

"Research on ethnic studies show that when students' identities are affirmed in the curriculum there is a direct increase in motivation and engagement with school." [101]

Dr. Tim San Pedro introduces the term and concept of sacred truth space, which "pushes the uncritical boundaries found when theorizing about the goals and outcomes of safe spaces in schools." These classrooms spaces are sacred and truth-seeking ones where Indigenous students and other students of colors are centered and their "ability to share their realities and experiences that counter/challenge/correct standard knowledge that leads to painful silencing experiences in schooling." In sacred truth spaces students act vulnerably and safety isn't necessarily the goal. Instead the goals include listening and learning from others. [102-103]

"Culture is not static, nor is it trapped in the past." [112]

Questions for reflection:

1. How do reading teachers center the White gaze in text selection and reading instruction? _____

_____

2. What would it look like for you not to align your expectations with White middle class norms of success? _____

_____

3. What are some ways to celebrate and honor linguistic diversity and dexterity?

_____

_____

4. How does your reading instruction operate as a site for sustaining the cultural ways of being of communities of the global majority?_____

_____

5. How can your reading instruction go beyond representation into affirmation of the identities of students of the global majority? _____

_____

_____

6. How does your reading instruction, through text selection, represent and affirm Indigenous identity? _____

_____

_____

7. How can your reading instruction be a sacred truth space?

_____

_____

8. In light of all this, what is your purpose in teaching?

_____

_____

_____

_____

"Suspending Damage"
REFLECTION EXERCISE

"Suspending Damage" was a letter Dr. Eve Tuck wrote (2009 Harvard Educational Review) to Native communities and communities of color with troubled relationships with researchers. She speaks of the concerns and problematic historic patterns in research and reports. Below are excerpts and important points that I think we can consider when it comes to reading instruction.

"The trouble comes from the historical exploitation and mistreatment of people and material. It also comes from feelings of being over researched yet, ironically, made invisible."

"For many of us, the research on our communities has historically been damage centered, intent on portraying our neighborhoods and tribes as defeated and broken."

"I believe that for many well-meaning people, it is actually a de facto reliance on a potentially problematic theory of change that leads to damage-centered research. In a damage-centered framework, pain and loss are documented in order to obtain particular political or material gains."

"As I will explore, desire-based research frameworks are concerned with understanding complexity, contradiction, and the self-determination of lived lives. Considering the excerpt from Craig Gingrich-Philbrook (2005), desire- based frameworks defy the lure to serve as "advertisements for power" by documenting not only the painful elements of social realities but also the wisdom and hope. Such an axiology is intent on depathologizing the experiences of dispossessed and disenfranchised communities so that people are seen as more than broken and conquered. This is to say that even when communities are broken and conquered, they are so much more than that—so much more that this incomplete story is an act of aggression."

"It is certainly not a call for another "d" word: denial. It is not a call to paint everything as peachy, as fine, as over."

Questions for reflection:

1. In what ways can your reading instruction help students develop a more complex understanding of Communities of the Global Majority?_____

_____

_____

2. What books and what reflection exercises can we assemble for students so that they can explore a more complete story of resilience and joy as it relates to Communities of the Global Majority?_____

_____

_____

3. In our efforts to promote and inspire empathy in students, how may we have pushed for a damage-centered narrative through our text selections?_____

_____

_____

4. In what ways have you/can you address how literature has historically portrayed People of the Global Majority and their communities as defeated and broken?

_____

_____

_____

_____

Playing in the Dark
REFLECTION EXERCISE

Toni Morrison, winner of the Nobel Prize in Literature, was a critical theorist and deep literary creator. She is the author of the concept 'White gaze' and a woman whose writing and life perspective are admirable. Her recent death has left and irreplaceable void. The publication, Playing in the Dark: Whiteness and the Literary Imagination (1992 Vintage Books) is a gift to us for rethinking and engaging in the conversation about race, racism, and Whiteness in literature. While there is so much to elicit from this book, I want us to focus on two main ideas. The first is the idea about the presence of racial silence in literature. The second is about how race and racism have impacted the racist individual, versus our constant preoccupation with only analyzing how it's impacted the oppressed. Below are excerpts from her book, followed by reflection questions.

"There seems to be a more or less tacit agreement among literary scholars that, because American literature has been clearly the preserve of White male views, genius, and power, those views, genius and power are without relationship to and removed from the overwhelming presence of black people in the United States. This agreement is made about a population that preceded every American writer of renown… The contemplation of this black presence is central to any understanding of our national literature and should not be permitted to hover at the margins of the literary imagination." [5]

"These speculations have led me to wonder whether the major and championed characteristics of our national literature- individualism, masculinity, social engagement versus historical isolation; acute and ambiguous moral problematics; the thematics of innocence coupled with an obsession with figurations of death and hell- are not in fact responses to a dark, abiding, signing Africanist presence." [5]

"Just as the formation of the nation necessitated coded language and purposeful restriction to deal with the racial disingenuousness and moral frailty at its heart, so too did the literature, whose founding characteristics extend into the twentieth century, reproduce the necessity for codes and restriction. Through significant and underscored omissions, startling contradictions, heavily nuanced conflicts, through the way writers peopled their work with the signs and bodies of this presence- one can see that a real or fabricated Africanist presence was crucial to their sense of Americanness. And it shows." [6]

"... in matters of race, silence and evasion have historically ruled literary discourse." [9]

"My early assumptions as a reader were that black people signified little or nothing in the imagination of White American writers... This was a reflection, I thought, of the marginal impact that blacks had on the lives of the characters in the work as well as the creative imagination of the author." [15]

Questions for reflection:

1. How has your text selection and curricula maintained the silence and avoidance of Blackness, Indigeneity, and other marginalized groups in literature?

_____

_____

2. Would you agree that the characteristics listed in the quote above (individualism, masculinity, social engagement versus historical isolation; acute and ambiguous moral problematics; the thematics of innocence coupled with an obsession with figurations of death and hell) are aspects of U.S. national literature? If so, how do they relate to or reflect traits of White Supremacy?_____

_____

_____

3. Have matters of race, silence, and evasion historically ruled literary discourse in your classes? If so, how do you plan to change that? If not, how can you go deeper?

_____

_____

4. How might your instruction have led students to believe that Black people have had little impact on the imagination, or been absent from the imagination, of White American authors?

_____

_____

_____

_____

Citizen
REFLECTION EXERCISE

Claudia Rankine, poet of Jamaican heritage, who's published several works, also published Citizen: An American Lyric (2014 Graywolf Press). It can be described as both criticism and poetry. There are two pieces, specifically, that we can use to think about anti-racist reading instruction. Below are the excerpts followed by reflection questions.

Poem 1
Because white men can't
Police their imagination
Black men are dying.

Figure 1

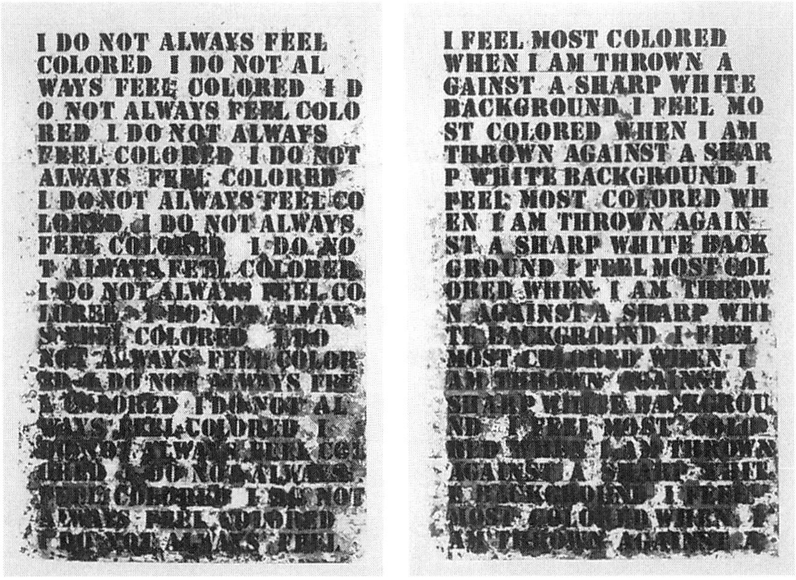

Questions for reflection:

1. How is your reading instruction helping students police their imaginations? What does that look like? _____

_____

_____

2. How might your curriculum create a white background where your students of the global majority feel "most colored"? _____

_____

_____

3. How might our books and text selections "throw" students against a "sharp" white background? What makes that white background "sharp"?

_____

_____

_____

_____

How to Be An Antiracist
REFLECTION EXERCISE

Award-winning author Ibram Kendi, published How to Be An Antiracist (2019 One World) and in it he outlines racist and antiracist ideology. He walks us through areas of our lives and society and points to the racist ideologies at their core.

"Assimilationist ideas are racist ideas. Assimilationists can position any racial group as the superior standard that another racial group should be measuring themselves against, the benchmark they should be trying to reach. Assimilationists typically position White people as the superior standard." (29)

> A racist idea is any idea that suggests one racial group is inferior or superior to another racial group in any way.

"Assimilationist ideas an segregationist ideas are the two types of racist ideas, the duel within racist thought…. Assimilationists believe that people of color can, in fact, be developed, become fully human, just like White people. Assimilationist ideas reduce people of color to the level of children needing instruction on how to act… Segregationist ideas cast people of color as "animals," to use Trump's descriptor for Latinx immigrants- unteachable after a point." (31)

"Antiracist ideas are based on the truth that racial groups are equals in all the ways they are different, assimilationist ideas are rooted in the notion that certain racial groups are culturally or behaviorally inferior, and segregationist ideas spring from a belief in genetic racial distinction and fixed hierarchy." (31)

"White people have generally advocated for both assimilationist and segregationist policies. People of color have generally advocated for both antiracist and assimilationist policies." (32)

Questions for reflection:

1. How might our curriculum and text selection further assimilationist or segregationist ideology? _____

_____

_____

2. How might our expectations of success be rooted in assimilationist ideology?

_____

_____

3. What could conquering the "assimilationist consciousness" and the "segregationist consciousness" look like in reading instruction?

_____

_____

_____

_____

Anti Racist Reading Instruction
STRATEGIES & TIPS

How we enact an anti racist reading pedagogy is nuanced and challenging. Many aspects of our teaching are contextual and based on the students sitting in front of us. Here are some specific strategies to explore.

Pausing & discussing

Considering that individuality/isolation and quantity over quality are traits of White Supremacy culture, disrupting those patterns is good work. Therefore, stopping in the midst of reading in order to pause, gather ourselves, and discuss is both good teaching practice, but also anti-racist IF you are intentional. When you pause, you want to intentionally build students' consciousness and critical thinking about what they're reading, what is missing, and what they need to draw out. Here are some questions that can guide that discussion:

- **What voices are pervasive in this text and why do you think that is?**
- **Does that voice represent dominant ideals in our culture?**
- **What perspective is missing and how is it impacting the plot? The characters? The conflict?**
- **How do issues of race, ethnicity, and identity directly and indirectly present themselves in this text?**
- **How are People of the Global Majority treated in this text? If absent, what might that suggest about the text and the author?**

Focusing on minor characters

Often, in novels, minor characters are People of the Global Majority. Too often they aren't the protagonists, but exist as minor characters playing marginal roles. In such cases, granting them some curriculum time is key to helping students see these characters, understand them, and make observations about their presence. Here are some tips for constructing these activities:

Consider a minor character that heavily impacts plot, the protagonist, or the conflict but is overlooked.	Spend a day discussing their role in the plot and consider the story without them. Discussion questions: • How does the plot change when they're missing? • What value does this character bring to the story? • How might that reflect the author's beliefs?
After defining 'racial token', help students consider a minor character that is tokenized.	Discussion questions: • How are these characters tokenized to serve the White characters? • How do these tokenized characters support a White gaze (Morrison)? • Explore with students what this character could do to break out of this tokenized role. Imagine how that might change the plot and other characters.
Consider a minor character that employs a stereotype.	Discuss the stereotype that the character is performing and how that serves the other characters in the story. Discussion questions: • Does the stereotype support White Supremacist ideas? • Does it maintain a racist status quo? • How does this stereotype allow other characters to get away with particular behaviors or choices? • How does this stereotype, and its presentation in the text, communicate the values of the author/writer?

Building a counternarrative

One way to have intentional and explicit anti-racist conversations is to build a counternarrative with and for students. The texts and materials you do choose, should overwhelmingly, if not all, be written from the perspective of members of that community. A counternarrative can offer a healthy and holistic understanding of groups of people. This can be accomplished by identifying the stereotypes held against people groups, and creating units of study that deliberately offer alternate views. For example, there exists a stereotype about Black men as animalistic, barbaric, and violent. Building a counternarrative could include creating a text set where Black men are protagonists and involved in tender, honest, and loving relationships of all kinds. It would require showing Black men as gentle fathers, loving husbands, emotional brothers, dependable friends, queer people, and more. You would start the unit by having the explicit conversation about the stereotype and then introducing the texts the class will be engaging in as a more holistic understanding of Black men. Below I've included a chart with two examples.

RACIAL STEREOTYPE	TEXTS FOR A COUNTERNARRATIVE
Black men as animalistic & violent	*Heavy* (Laymon), *Ghost* (Reynolds), Doc McStuffins episodes, Philadelphia film, R & B singers: Babyface, Tevin Campbell, Boyz II Men
Latinas as sexy and fierce	Real Women Have Curves film, *In the Time of the Butterflies* (Alvarez), *The Poet X* (Acevedo), *With the Fire on High* (Acevedo), *The House on Mango Street* (Cisneros), Jane the Virgin episodes

Teaching socio political context

I can't stress this strategy enough. This practice involves helping students see the word in the midst of the world and their role in that transaction. It is necessary because it allows students to understand the impact of their identity on their comprehension and analysis. It allows them to understand how reading and writing do not occur in a vacuum, but they are communal, both physically and socially. I encourage that you start with having students explore their own identity and positionality. Then, you can welcome them into a dialogue where they look outside of themselves. Here are some questions to guide that conversation with students:

- What impact does our current political context have on my interpretation of this text?
- Why does the time period when this text was written matter to me as a reader?
- How does the author's racial identity impact the content?
- How does my racial and ethnic identity impact my reading and interpretation of this text?
- How might popular culture impact my analysis of this text, what I notice and don't notice?
- Is there any trace of colonialism in this text and how might that be related to the author's identity?

You can easily ask questions about social class, partisan ideas, and/or gender, too. Disrupting the silence around these topics is key to establishing a classroom space that is open and honest. The point of this exercise and these discussions is to help students see themselves in new ways. For students of the global majority, this allows them to place themselves in larger social conversations and offers them language they can use to discuss their critical points of view. For White students, it helps them break the barrier of silence and avoidance and immediately forces introspection. It generates an awareness for students that will, hopefully, lead them to a better understanding of the world they're a part of.

Thank you!

The **The Anti Racist Teacher:** Reading Instruction Workbook wouldn't have been possible without the support of a whole crew of dedicated, loving, and hardworking people. My husband, Roberto, was instrumental in making it possible for me to complete this work for all of you. My sister, Francesca, was crucial in coaching me through the production of it all. My cousin Wanda came through with that cover design. My friend editors: Jineyda, Dan, Katie, Sarah, and Julia gave insight and suggested improvements. I'm eternally grateful.

I'm so excited for us and the work we have ahead. I hope that this workbook is helpful to you. I hope that these readings and these questions help us all to do better for the sake of our future.

My prayer is that this workbook will sustain the fire in our bellies. I want us to pay attention to all the details and know that our impact in the classroom is felt. Therefore, we need to make it count. Does our impact function to promote racial justice and liberation? Does your work in the classroom cause young people to value lives and not believe in killing? Does your teaching approach dismantle the hurt and pain historically caused by schooling? These are big questions and an important process. I'm honored to be on this journey together.

I hope that this workbook plays a role in our students becoming that change we always talk about wanting to see. The hands of White Supremacy have been choking us. They're killing Black and Brown people in this nation. They're murdering us, imprisoning us, failing us, pushing us out, and more. Those hands have created the poison that is rotting White America. Racism is hurting us all. I hope that this work really does help liberate us from the hands of White Supremacy.

¡Pa'lante en la lucha!

Made in the USA
Middletown, DE
25 October 2021

51016034R00026